green dream throw

Materials

Yarn ❹
RED HEART Soft Yarn, 5oz/140g skeins,
each approx 256yd/234m (acrylic)
• 4 skeins #4420 Guacamole (A)
• 2 skeins #9522 Leaf (B)
• 1 skein #9520 Seafoam (C)
• 1 skein #4412 Grass Green (D)

Crochet hook
• Size I/9 (5.5mm) crochet hook *or any size to obtain correct gauge*

Notions
• Yarn needle

Finished Measurements
Approx 33"/84cm x 43"/109cm

Gauge
Granny Square = 2½"/6.5cm square
Remember to check gauge for best results!

Stitch Glossary

beginning shell
Ch 3 (counts as dc),
2 dc in sp indicated.
shell Work 3 dc in sp indicated.
beginning corner shell
Work (ch 3, 2 dc, ch 1, 3 dc) in sp indicated.
corner shell Work (3 dc, ch 1, 3 dc) in sp indicated.

Throw

One Color Granny Square
(make 90 total: 65 with A, 9 with B, 8 with C and 8 with D)
Ch 4, join with sl st in first ch to form a ring.
Round 1 (right side) Work beginning shell in ring, ch 1 [shell in ring, ch 1] 3 times; join with sl st in 3rd ch of beginning shell—4 shells and 4 corner ch-1 sps. **Round 2** Sl st in next 2 dc, sl st in corner ch-1 sp, work beginning corner shell in same ch-1 sp, ch 1, [corner shell in next ch-1 sp, ch 1] 3 times; join with sl st in 3rd ch of beginning corner shell—4 corner shells. Fasten off.

Two Color Granny Square
(make 102 total: 5 with A/B, 5 with A/C, 5 with A/D, 19 with B/A, 5 with B/C, 5 with B/D, 19 with C/A, 5 with C/B, 5 with C/D, 19 with D/A, 5 with D/B and 5 with D/C)
Note Color listed before / is first color. Color listed after / is second color.
With first color, ch 4; join with sl st in first ch to form a ring.
Round 1 (right side) Work beginning shell in ring, ch 1 [shell in ring, ch 1] 3 times; join with sl st in 3rd ch of beginning shell—4 shells and 4 corner ch-1 sps. Fasten off. **Round 2** With right side facing, join second color with sl st in next ch-1 sp, work beginning corner shell in same ch-1 sp, ch 1, [corner shell in next ch-1 sp, ch 1] 3 times; join with sl st in 3rd ch of beginning corner shell—4 corner shells. Fasten off.

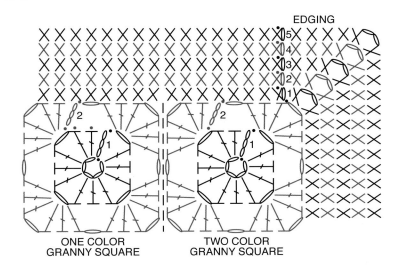

ONE COLOR
GRANNY SQUARE

TWO COLOR
GRANNY SQUARE

EDGING

Assembly

With right sides facing, arrange squares as desired. Using A, whipstitch squares tog into rows, working through back loops of corresponding sts on each square, starting and ending with ch in corners. Whipstitch rows tog, working through back loops of corresponding sts on each square.

Edging

Round 1 With right side facing, join A with sl st in any dc, ch 1, sc in same st as joining, sc in each dc and ch-1 sp around, skipping seams between squares and working (sc, ch 2, sc) in each corner ch-1 sp; join with sl st in first sc. Fasten off. **Round 2** With right side facing, join B with sl st in any sc, ch 1, sc in same st as joining, sc in each sc around, working (sc, ch 2, sc) in each corner ch-2 sp; join.
Fasten off.
Round 3 With C, repeat Round 2. **Round 4** With D, repeat Round 2. **Round 5** With A, repeat Round 2.

Finishing

Weave in all ends.

wrap-up afghan

Materials

Yarn ☐
RED HEART Soft Yarn, 5oz/140g balls, each approx 256yd/234m (acrylic)
• 3 balls #9114 Honey (A)
• 3 balls #4422 Tangerine (B)
• 3 balls #9520 Seafoam (C)
• 2 balls #9518 Teal (D)
• 4 balls #4614 Black (E)

Crochet hook
Size I/9 (5.5mm) crochet hook *or any size to obtain correct gauge*

Notions
Yarn needle

Finished Measurements
Approx 43"/109cm x 51½"/131cm

Gauge
Square = 8½"/21.5cm square
Remember to check gauge for best results!

Afghan

Square #1 (Make 10)
With A, ch 6; join with sl st to form a ring.

Round 1 (right side) Ch 3 (counts as dc here and throughout), 2 dc in ring, [ch 3, 3 dc in ring] 3 times, ch 3; join with sl st in 3rd ch of beginning ch-3—12 dc and 4 corner ch-3 sps. Fasten off.

Round 2 With right side facing, join B with sl st in any corner ch-3 sp, ch 5 (counts as dc and ch-2 sp here and throughout), *(3 dc, ch 3, 3 dc) in next corner ch-3 sp, ch 2; repeat from * 2 more times, (3 dc, ch 3, 2 dc) in first corner ch-3 sp; join with sl st in 3rd ch of beginning ch-5—24 dc, 4 corner ch-3 sps and 4 ch-2 sps.

Round 3 Sl st in next ch-2 sp, ch 3 (counts as dc here and throughout), 2 dc in same ch-2 sp, *ch 2, (3 dc, ch 3, 3 dc) in next corner ch-3 sp, ch 2**, 3 dc in next ch-2 sp; repeat from * 3 more times, ending last repeat at **; join with sl st in 3rd ch of beginning ch-3—36 dc, 4 corner ch-3 sps and 8 ch-2 sps.

Round 4 Ch 5, 3 dc in next ch-2 sp, *ch 2, (3 dc, ch 3, 3 dc) in next corner ch-3 sp**, [ch 2, 3 dc in next ch-2 sp] twice; repeat from * 3 more times, ending last repeat at **, ch 2, 2 dc in last ch-2 sp; join with sl st in 3rd ch of beginning ch-5—48 dc, 4 corner ch-3 sps and 12 ch-2 sps. Fasten off.

Round 5 With right side facing, join C with sl st in next ch-2 sp, ch 3, 2 dc in same ch-2 sp as joining, ch 2, 3 dc in next ch-2 sp, *ch 2, (3 dc, ch 3, 3 dc) in next corner ch-3 sp**, [ch 2, 3 dc in next ch-2 sp] 3 times; repeat from * 3 more times, ending last repeat at **, ch 2, 3 dc in last ch-2 sp, ch 2; join with sl st in 3rd ch of beginning ch-3—60 dc, 4 corner ch-3 sps, and 16 ch-2 sps. Fasten off.

Round 6 With right side facing, join D with sl st in same ch as joining, ch 1, sc in same ch as joining, sc in each dc, 2 sc in each ch-2 sp, and 3 sc in each corner ch-3 sp around; join with sl st in first sc—104 sc. Fasten off.

Round 7 With right side facing, join E with sl st in any sc, ch 3, dc in next sc and in each sc around, working (dc, ch 1, dc) in middle sc of 3 sc in each corner; join with sl st in 3rd ch of beginning ch-3—108 dc and 4 corner ch-1 sps.

Round 8 Ch 3, dc in each dc around, working (dc, ch 1, dc) in each corner ch-1 sp; join with sl st in 3rd ch of beginning ch-3—112 dc and 4 corner ch-1 sps. Fasten off.

Square #2 (Make 10)
Work same as Square #1 with the following color sequence: D, C, B, A, E.

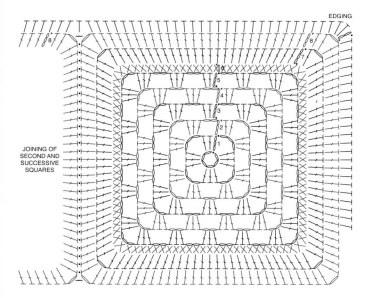

EDGING

JOINING OF
SECOND AND
SUCCESSIVE
SQUARES

Square #3 (Make 10)
Work same as Square #1 with the following color sequence: B, A, D, C, E.

Assembly

Following Assembly Chart, arrange squares into 5 rows with 6 squares in each row as follows: With right sides of 2 squares together, using E and working through both thicknesses, sl st in both loops of each st across squares, starting and ending at corner ch-1 sps. Join all squares together into rows. Join rows together in same manner.

Edging

With right side facing, join A with sl st in any corner ch-1 sp, ch 2 (counts as hdc), 2 hdc in same ch-sp as joining, *hdc in each st and in each square joining across to next corner**, 3 hdc in next corner ch-1 sp; repeat from * 3 more times, ending last repeat at **; join with sl st in 2nd ch of beginning ch-2.
Fasten off.

1	2	3	1	2
3	1	2	3	1
2	3	1	2	3
1	2	3	1	2
3	1	2	3	1
2	3	1	2	3

Assembly Diagram

Finishing

Weave in all ends. Block if necessary.

good cause afghan

Rose Callahan

Materials

Yarn ④
RED HEART Super Saver,
7oz/198g skeins, each
approx. 364yd/333m (acrylic)
1 skein each:
- #330 Linen (A)
- #668 Honeydew (B)
- #656 Real Teal (C)
- #376 Burgundy (D)
- #332 Ranch Red (E)

Crochet hook
Size J/10 (6mm) crochet hook
*or any size to obtain correct
gauge*

Notions
- Yarn needle

Finished Measurements
Approx 44"/111.5cm x
61"/155cm

Gauge
Motif = 8½"/21.5cm square
*Remember to check gauge
for best results!*

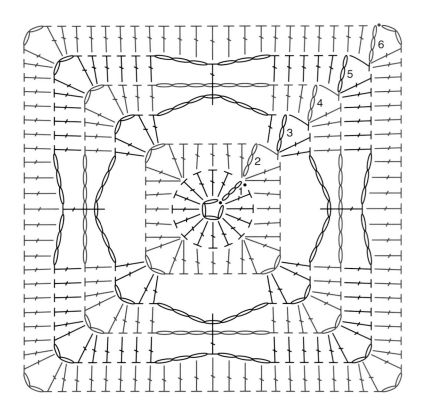

Stitch Glossary

Long dc Yarn over, insert hook in indicated st, yarn over and draw up a loop to approx ½"/1.3cm tall, [yarn over and draw through 2 loops on hook] twice

Afghan

Motif (make 7 with each color)

With appropriate color, ch 4; join with sl st in first ch to form a ring.

Round 1 (right side) Ch 3 (counts as dc now and throughout), 15 dc in ring; join with sl st in 3rd ch of beginning ch-3—16 dc.

Round 2 Ch 3, dc in same ch as joining; *dc in next 3 dc, [2 dc, ch 2, 2 dc] in next dc (corner made); repeat from * 2 more times; dc in next 3 dc, 2 dc in same ch as beginning ch-3; join with hdc in 3rd ch of beginning ch-3 (counts as ch-2 sp of last corner)—28 dc and 4 corner ch-2 sps.

Round 3 (Sl st, ch 3, dc) around post of joining hdc; *ch 7, sk next 7 dc, [2 dc, ch 2, 2 dc] in next corner ch-2 sp; repeat from * 2 more times; ch 7, sk next 7 dc, 2 dc around post of joining hdc; join with hdc in 3rd ch of beginning ch-3—16 dc, 4 ch-7 sps and 4 corner ch-2 sps.

Round 4 (Sl st, ch 3, dc) around post of joining hdc; *dc in next 2 dc, ch 7, sk next ch-7 sp, dc in next 2 dc**; [2 dc, ch 2, 2 dc] in next corner ch-2 sp; repeat from * 3 more times, ending last repeat at **; 2 dc around post of joining hdc; join with hdc in 3rd ch of beginning ch-3—32 dc, 4 ch-7 sps and 4 corner ch-2 sps.

Round 5 (Sl st, ch 3, dc) around post of joining hdc; *dc in next 4 dc, ch 3; working over both ch-7 sps, work long dc in center dc of 7 skipped dc on round 2; ch 3, dc in next 4 dc**; [2 dc, ch 2, 2 dc] in next corner ch-2 sp; repeat from * 3 more times, ending last repeat at **; 2 dc around post of joining hdc; join with hdc in 3rd ch of beginning ch-3—4 long dc, 48 dc, 8 ch-3 sps and 4 corner ch-2 sps.

Round 6 (Sl st, ch 3, dc) around post of joining hdc; *dc in next 6 dc, 3 dc in next ch-3 sp, dc in next long dc, 3 dc in next ch-3 sp, dc in next 6 dc**; [2 dc, ch 2, 2 dc] in next corner ch-2 sp; repeat from * 3 more times, ending last repeat at **; 2 dc around post of joining hdc, ch 2; join with sl st in 3rd ch of beginning ch-3—92 dc and 4 corner ch-2 sps. Fasten off.

Assembly

With right sides facing, arrange motifs randomly, or as desired, in 7 rows of 5 motifs each. With right sides of 2 motifs together and color of choice, working through both thicknesses and matching sts, sl st through back loops of each st across, starting and ending with one ch in each corner. Join remaining motifs in same manner into rows, then join rows together.

Edging

With right side facing, join color of choice with sl st in back loop of any dc around edge, ch 3 (counts as dc), dc in back loop of next dc and in back loop of each dc around, working 2 dc in each ch of 4 corner ch-2 sps.

Finishing
Weave in all ends.

Tip
To make the edging stronger, work dc into back loop and back bar of each st around.

Stitch for a cause
Simple, easy-to-crochet motifs make this blanket the perfect thing to donate to a charity organization. For speedy results, stitch it up with friends! Gather a small group of people (anywhere from 2 to 10), name the date and place, and gather the necessary yarn. Make a few squares each, and in no time you'll have enough for a full afghan. You can even sew it up together and take turns stitching on the edging. So go ahead—invite your friends and their hooks, gather some worsted weight yarn, and have a fun night of stitching for a good cause!

Once your blanket is finished, there are many organizations that would be grateful to have it. Here are just a few to consider:

- Afghans for Afghans sends hand-stitched blankets to the needy of Afghanistan.
  www.afghansforafghans.org
- Blankets for the Gulf distributes blankets to the still struggling victims of Hurricane Katrina.
  www.blanketsforthegulf.com
- Warming Families is looking for warm items—especially blankets—to help homeless and displaced families living in shelters.
  www.warmingfamilies.com
- Friends of the Pine Ridge Reservation is always looking for warm handmade items for the large population at the Reservation.
  www.friendsofpineridgereservation.org

blue skies blanket

Materials

Yarn ⓸
RED HEART Super Saver, 7oz/198g skeins, each approx 364yd/333m (acrylic)
- 2 skeins #0320 Cornmeal (A)
- 2 skeins #0885 Delft Blue (B)
- 2 skeins #0381 Light Blue (C)
- 2 skeins #0387 Soft Navy (D)

Crochet hook
Size I/9 (5.5mm) crochet hook *or any size to obtain correct gauge*

Notions
Yarn needle

Finished Measurements
Approx 53"/134.6cm wide x 67"/170cm long

Gauge
Rounds 1–4 of Square = 6"/15cm diameter
1 Square (including joining border) = 8½ x 8½"/21.6cm x 21.6cm using size I/9 (5.5mm) crochet hook.
Remember to check gauge for best results.

Stitch Glossary
slanted-group Ch 3, 3 dc around post of dc just made.

Blanket
SQUARE 1 (make 20)
Work squares in the following color sequence: Work Rounds 1 and 2 with A, Rounds 3 and 4 with B, and Rounds 5–7 with D. With first color, ch 4; join with sl st in first ch to form a ring.
Round 1 Ch 1, work 16 sc in ring; join with sl st in first sc—16 sc.
Round 2 Ch 5 (counts as hdc, ch 3), *sk next st, hdc in next st, ch 3; repeat from * around; join with sl st in 2nd ch of beginning ch—8 hdc and 8 ch-3 spaces. Fasten off first color.
Round 3 Join 2nd color with sl st in any ch-3 space, ch 3 (counts as dc), 3 dc in same space, *sk next st, 4 dc in next ch-3 space; repeat from * around; join with sl st in top of beginning ch—32 dc.
Round 4 Ch 3, dc in same st as join, work slanted-group around dc just made and beginning ch (hold dc and beginning ch together and work around both at the same time), sk next dc, [dc in next dc, work slanted-group around dc just made, sk next dc] 15 times; join with sl st in top of beginning ch—16 slanted-groups. Fasten off 2nd color.
Round 5 Join third color in top of ch-3 of any slanted-group, ch 8 (counts as tr, ch 4), sc in top of next ch-3, [ch 4, sc in top of next ch-3] 2 times, [ch 4, (tr, ch 4, tr) in top of next ch-3 (corner made), (ch 4, sc in top of next ch-3) 3 times] 3 times, ch 4, tr in base of beginning ch; join with ch 2, hdc in 4th ch of beginning ch (counts as ch-4 space)—8 tr, 12 sc, and 20 ch-4 spaces.
Round 6 Ch 2, turn, 3 hdc in space just made (formed by ch-2, hdc join of previous round), [4 hdc in next 4 ch-4 spaces, (4 hdc, ch 3, 4 hdc) in next ch-4 space (corner)] 3 times, 4 hdc in next 4 ch-4 spaces, 4 hdc in beginning space; join with ch 2, hdc in top of beginning ch—4 ch-4 space, and 24 hdc on each side.
Round 7 Ch 2, turn, hdc in space just made (formed by ch-2, hdc join of previous round), [hdc in next 24 hdc, (2 hdc, ch 3, 2 hdc) in next ch-3 space (corner)] 3 times, hdc in next 24 hdc, 2 hdc in beginning space, ch 3; join with sl st in top of beginning ch—4 ch-3 spaces, and 28 hdc on each side. Fasten off 3rd color.

SQUARE 2 (make 12)
Work as for Square 1 in the following color sequence: Work Rounds 1 and 2 with D, Rounds 3 and 4 with B, and Rounds 5–7 with C.

HALF SQUARE (make 14)
With D, ch 4; join with sl st in first ch to form a ring.
Row 1 (right side) Ch 1, work 9 sc in ring.
Row 2 Ch 5 (counts as hdc, ch 3), turn, sk next sc, hdc in next sc, [ch 3, sk next sc, hdc in next sc] 3 times—5 hdc and 4 ch-3 spaces. Fasten off D.
With right side facing, join B in top of first hdc.
Row 3 (right side) Ch 3 (counts as dc), 3 dc in next ch-3 space, [sk next hdc, 4 dc in next ch-3 space] 3 times, dc in 2nd ch of turning ch—17 dc.
Row 4 Ch 3 (counts as dc), turn, dc in same st, work slanted-group around dc just made, [sk next st, dc in next st, work slanted-group around dc just made] 8 times—9 slanted-groups. Fasten off B.
With right side facing join C in top of first ch-3.
Row 5 (right side) Ch 8 (counts as dtr, ch 3), tr in same st (corner), [ch 4, sc in top of next ch-3] 3 times, ch 4, (tr, ch 3, tr) in next ch-3 (corner), [ch 4, sc in top of next ch-3] 3 times, ch 4, (tr, ch 3, dtr) in last ch-3 (for corner)—3 corners, 6 sc, 8 ch-4 spaces.

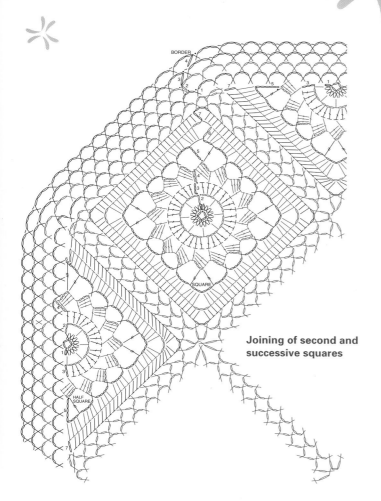

Joining of second and
successive squares

Row 6 Ch 1, turn, sl st in first ch-3 space, ch 2 (counts as hdc), 3 hdc in same ch-3 space, 4 hdc in next 4 ch-4 spaces, (4 hdc, ch 3, 4 hdc) in next ch-3 space (corner), 4 hdc in next 4 ch-4 spaces, 3 hdc in next ch-3 space (corner), hdc in 5th ch of turning ch—1 ch-3 space, 24 hdc on each side.

Row 7 Ch 2, turn, hdc in each hdc to ch-3 space, (4 hdc, ch 3, 4 hdc) in ch-3 space (corner), hdc in each hdc to end—1 ch-3 space and 28 hdc on each side.

Finishing

Join squares

A ch-3 border is worked around the first square. As the border is worked around the next square, the ch-3's are joined along one or more edges. Refer to the assembly diagram to determine which squares and edges to join. Join the full squares first then join the half squares.

First square

With right side facing, join A with sc in any corner ch-3 space.
Round 1 Ch 3, sc in same ch-3 space, ch 3, sk next 3 sts, sc in next st, [ch 3, sk next 2 sts, sc in next st] 7 times, ch 3, sk next 3 sts, *(sc, ch 3, sc) in corner ch-3 space, ch 3, sk next 3 sts, sc in next st, [ch 3, sk next 2 sts, sc in next st] 7 times, ch 3, sk next 3 sts; repeat from * around; join with sl st in first sc. Fasten off.

Next squares

With right side facing, join A with sc in any corner ch-3 space. Work border, as for first square, around non-joining edges. Join edge(s) to neighbor squares according to assembly diagram. To join an edge, begin with sc in ch-3 space, and work as follows.

Joining edge

Ch 1, sc in corresponding corner ch-3 space of previous square(s), ch 1, sc in same corner ch-3 space of current square; ch 1, sc in next ch-3 space of previous square, ch 1, sk next 3 sts of current square, *sc in next st of current square, ch 1, sc in next ch-3 space of previous square(s), ch 1, sk next 2 sts of current square; repeat from * across to next corner ch-3 space of current square, sc in corner ch-3 space of current square.
Join all squares according to assembly diagram.

Join half square

Position half block as shown in assembly diagram. With right side facing, join A with sc in side corner space of half square.
Round 1 Ch 1, sc in corresponding corner space of previous square, ch 1, sc in same corner space of current half square, *ch 1, sc in next ch-3 space of previous square, ch 1, sk next 3 sts of current half square, sc in next st of current half square, [ch 1, sc in next ch-3 space of previous square, ch 1, sk next 2 sts of current half square, sc in next st of current half square] 7 times, ch 1, sc in next ch-3 space of previous square, ch 1, sk next 3 sts of current half square, sc in corner ch-3 space of current half square, ch 1, sc in corresponding corner space of previous square(s), ch 1, sc in same corner space of current half square; repeat from * one more time. Fasten off. Leave long edge of half square unworked.

Border

With right side facing, join A in first corner ch-3 space of corner square,

Round 1 *Working across edge of corner square, [ch 3, sk next sc, sc in next ch-3 space] 9 times; ch 3, sc in join between square and half square; working along edges of half squares, work (ch 3, sc in end of row) evenly spaced across to next corner square, ch 3, sc in ch-3 space of corner square; repeat from * 3 more times, omit last sc of last repetition; join with sl st in first sc.

Round 2 Sl st in next ch-3 space, ch 1, sc in same space, ch 3, sk next sc, *sc in next ch-3 space, ch 3, sk next sc; repeat from * around; join with sl st in first sc.

Round 3 Working in opposite direction from usual, ch 1, rev sc in first ch-3 space, *ch 3, sk next sc, rev sc in next ch-3 space; repeat from * around, ch 3; join with sl st in first sc. Fasten off.

Round 4 Join D with sc in any ch-3 space; working in opposite direction from usual, *ch 3, sk next sc, rev sc in next ch-3 space; repeat from * around, ch 3; join with sl st in first sc. Fasten off. Weave in all ends.

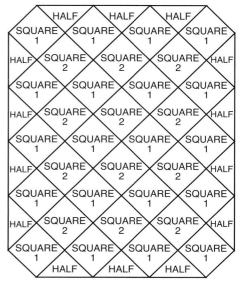

Construction Diagram

mosaic granny

MATERIALS

Yarn ❹

RED HEART *Super Saver,* 7oz/198g skeins, each approx 364yd/333m (acrylic)
- 3 skeins #360 Café (H)

1 skein each in:
- #341 Light Grey (A)
- #387 Soft Navy (B)
- #406 Medium Thyme (C)
- #378 Claret (D)
- #321 Gold (E)
- #256 Carrot (F)
- #776 Dark Orchid (G)

RED HEART Fiesta, 6oz/170g skeins, each approx 330yd/302m (acrylic/nylon), 1 skein each in:
- #6013 Wheat (I)
- #6012 Black (J)

Crochet hook

Size I/9 (5.5mm) crochet hook *or any size to obtain correct gauge*

Notions

Yarn needle

FINISHED MEASUREMENTS

46"/117cm x 65"/165cm

GAUGE

Rounds 1–3 in pattern = 2½"/6cm x 3½"/9cm

Remember to check gauge for best results.

Afghan

Note Refer to Color Sequence Chart to determine colors used on each round of each motif. Make 24 motifs as follows:

Motif 1 (make 4) Work Basic Motif through Round 6.
Motif 2 (make 4) Work Basic Motif through Round 6.
Motif 3 (make 3) Work Basic Motif through Round 7.
Motif 4 (make 3) Work Basic Motif through Round 7.
Motif 5 (make 2) Work Basic Motif through Round 9.
Motif 6 (make 2) Work Basic Motif through Round 9.
Motif 7 (make 2) Work Basic Motif through Round 10.
Motif 8 (make 2) Work Basic Motif through Round 10.
Motif 9 (make 2) Work Basic Motif through Round 10.

Basic Motif

Ch 5, join with sl st in first ch to form a ring.

Round 1 Ch 1, 10 sc in ring, join with sl st in first ch—10 sc.

Round 2 (Ch 4, sl st in next sc) 9 times, ch 4, sl st in first ch—10 ch-4 sp.

Round 3 Ch 1, (sc, ch 3, sc) in first ch-4 sp; *(2 dc, ch 3, 2 dc) in next ch-4 sp, (sc, ch 3, sc) in next ch-4 sp, (2 dc, ch 3, 2 dc) in next ch-4 sp*, (sc, ch 3, sc) in each of next 2 ch-4 sps; repeat from * to *; (sc, ch 3, sc) in last ch-4 sp; sl sl in first sc—10 ch-3 sp.

Round 4 Ch 1, sc in first ch-3 sp; *ch 4, (sc, ch3, sc) in next ch-3 sp, ch 4, sc in next ch-3 sp, ch 4, (sc, ch3, sc) in next ch-3 sp, ch 4, sc in next ch-3 sp, ch 2*, sc in next ch-3 sp; repeat from * to *; sl st to first sc- 2 ch-2 sp, 4 ch-3 sp, and 8 ch-4 sp. Fasten off. With right side facing, attach next color in sequence with sl st to either ch-2 sp.

Round 5 Ch 3 (counts as first dc), 2 dc in same sp as joining; *ch 1, 3 dc in next ch-4 sp, ch 1, (3 dc, ch 2, 3 dc) in next ch-3 sp; (ch 1, 3 dc) in each of next 2 ch-4 sps, ch 1, (3 dc, ch 2, 3 dc) in next ch-3 sp, ch 1, 3 dc in next ch-4 sp, ch 1*, 3 dc in next ch-2 sp; repeat from * to *, join with sl st to first dc—54 dc, 14 ch-1 sp and 4 ch-2 sp. Fasten off.

With wrong side facing, attach next color in sequence with sl st to the first ch-1 to the left of any corner.

Round 6 Ch 3, 2 dc in same sp as joining, *ch 1, (3 dc, ch 2, 3 dc) in next ch-2 sp, (ch 1, 3 dc) in each ch-1 space across to next corner; repeat from * around to first dc, ch 1, sl st in first dc; turn.

Round 7 With right side facing, attach next color in sequence to first ch-1 sp, repeat Round 6.

Round 8 With wrong side facing, attach next color in sequence to first ch-1 sp, repeat Round 6.

Rounds 9 and 10 Repeat Rounds 7 and 8.

All Motifs

Last Round With right side facing, join H with sl st to the first ch-1 to the left of any corner, ch 3, 2 dc in same sp as joining, *(ch 1, 3 dc) in each ch-1 sp to next corner ch-2 sp, ch 1, (3 dc, ch 3, 3 dc) in next ch-2 sp; repeat from * around to first dc, ch 1, sl st in first dc. Fasten off.

Assembly

Weave in ends. Arrange motifs as shown in construction chart. With H, whipstitch through back lps of sts joining motifs to create 4 panels as shown in chart.

Finishing

With right side facing of an inner panel, attach H with a sl st in any corner ch-3 sp.

Edging row Ch 1, 2 sc in same ch-3 sp as joining, *sc in each dc and ch-1 sp across to next ch-3 sp, 2 sc in ch-3 sp**, sc in seam, 2 sc in next ch-3 sp; repeat from * across, ending at ** in last ch-3 sp—219 sc. Fasten off. Repeat finishing row across inner edge of each panel. With H, whipstitch through back lps to join 4 panels following construction chart for placement.

Border

With right side facing, attach H with sl st to the first ch-1 to the left of any corner.

Round 1 Ch 3, 2 dc in same sp as joining, *(ch 1, 3 dc) in each ch-1 sp and each joined ch-3 sp across to next corner ch-3 sp, ch 1, (3 dc, ch 3, 3 dc) in next ch-3 sp; repeat from * around to last st, ch 1, sl st in first dc.

Round 2 Ch 1, *sc in each dc and ch-1 sp across to next corner, (sc, ch 3, sc) in next ch-3 sp; repeat from * around, ending with sc in each of last 4 sts, sl st in first sc.

Round 3 Ch 1, turn; sc in next sc, *(ch 3, sk 3 sc, sc in next sc) across** to next corner ch-3 sp, (sc, ch 3, sc) in next ch-3 sp, sc in next sc; repeat from * around, ending at **, ch 3, sl st in first sc.

Round 4 Ch 1, turn; sc in next ch-3 sp, *5 dc in next sc, sc in next ch-3 sp**; repeat from * to ** to last 2 sc before corner ch-3 sp; 5 dc in next sc, sc in next sc, 5 dc in ch-3 sp, sc in next sc; repeat from * around, ending at **, 5 dc in next sc, sl st in first sc. Fasten off. Weave in ends. With wrong side facing, block border lightly.

Basic Motif Diagram

MOTIFS		COLORS							
MOTIF #	# TO MAKE	RNDS 1-4	RND 5	RND 6	RND 7	RND 8	RND 9	RND 10	LAST RND
1	4	I	J	C	–	–	–	–	H
2	4	F	B	D	–	–	–	–	H
3	3	H	C	E	J	–	–	–	H
4	3	A	G	F	I	–	–	–	H
5	2	I	J	C	D	A	B	–	H
6	2	A	G	F	E	E	I	–	H
7	2	A	G	F	E	E	D	D	H
8	2	H	C	E	B	G	F	F	H
9	2	F	B	D	A	G	J	J	H

Color sequence chart

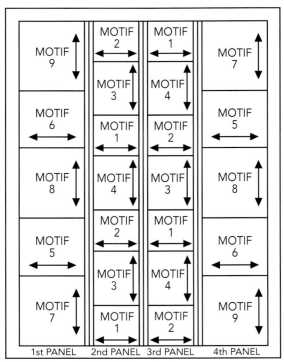

Construction chart
Note: Arrows indicate direction of wider dimension

blushing grannies

MATERIALS

Yarn ④

RED HEART *Super Saver*, 7oz/198g skeins, each approx
364yds/333m (acrylic)
- 1 skein #0332 Ranch Red (A)
- 1 skein #0376 Burgundy (B)
- 2 skeins #0378 Claret (C)

Crochet hook

Size I/9 (5.5mm) crochet hook *or any size to obtain correct gauge*

Notions

Yarn needle

FINISHED MEASUREMENTS

Approx 36"/91.5cm x 50"/127cm

GAUGE

Rounds 1–3 of square = 3½" x 3½"/9cm x 9cm
Full square = 6¾" x 6¾"/17cm x 17cm
Remember to check gauge for best results!

Square (make 35)

With A, ch 5. Join with sl st in first ch to form a ring.

Round 1 Ch 3 (counts as dc), work 15 dc in ring; join with sl st in 3rd ch of beginning ch-3—16 dc.

Round 2 Ch 1, sc in same ch as joining; *ch 4, sk next dc**; sc in next dc; repeat from * around, ending final repeat at **; join with sl st in first sc—8 sc and 8 ch-4 sps.

Round 3 Ch 1, sc in same sc as joining; *2 sc in next ch-4 sp, (2 dc, ch 2, 2 dc) in next sc, 2 sc in next ch-4 sp**; sc in next sc; repeat from * around, ending final repeat at **; join with sl st in first sc—20 sc, 16 dc and 4 corner ch-2 sps. Fasten off A.

Round 4 Join B with sl st in any corner ch-2 sp, ch 3 (counts as dc), (dc, ch 2, 2 dc) in same ch-2 sp as joining; *dc in next 9 sts**; (2 dc, ch 2, 2 dc) in next corner ch-2 sp; repeat from * around, ending final repeat at **; join with sl st in 3rd ch of beginning ch-3—52 dc and 4 corner ch-2 sps.

Round 5 *Ch 2, sk next dc, (sl st, ch 2, sl st) in next corner ch-2 sp**; (ch 2, sk next dc, sl st in next dc) 6 times; repeat from * around, ending final repeat at **; (ch 2, sk next dc, sl st in next dc) 5 times; ch 2, sk next dc; join with sl st in joining sl st—32 sl sts and 32 ch-2 sps. Fasten off B.

Round 6 Join C with sl st in any corner ch-2 sp, ch 3 (counts as dc), (dc, ch 2, 2 dc) in same ch-2 sp as joining; *2 dc in each of next 7 ch-2 sps**; (2 dc, ch 2, 2 dc) in next corner ch-2 sp; repeat from * around, ending final repeat at **; join with sl st in 3rd ch of beginning ch-3—72 dc and 4 corner ch-2 sps.

Round 7 Ch 1, sc in same ch as joining, sc in next dc; *(sc, ch 2, sc) in next corner ch-2 sp**; sc in next 18 dc; repeat from * around, ending final repeat at **; sc in last 16 dc; join with sl st in first sc—80 sc and 4 corner ch-2 sps. Fasten off C, leaving a long end for sewing.

Finishing

Weave in all loose ends, except long end. Sew squares together through both lps of last round into 5 rows of 7 squares each. Sew rows together.

Edging

Round 1 Join C with sc in any sc on edge of afghan, sc in next sc and in each sc around all 4 edges of afghan, working 2 sc in each ch-2 sp at corners of joined squares and 3 sc in each of 4 corner ch-2 sps of afghan; join with sl st in first sc—532 sc.

Round 2 Ch 1, sc in same sc as joining; *ch 3, sk next sc, sc in next sc; repeat from * around; join with sl st in first sc—266 sc and 266 ch-3 sps.

Round 3 *Work 2 sc in next ch-3 sp, sl st in next sc; repeat from * around, ending final repeat with sl st in joining sl st—532 sc and 266 sl sts. Fasten off. Weave in ends.

Tip

Use your leftover yarn to make matching pillows! Work two small squares or rectangles, crochet them together along 3 edges, stuff a pillow form inside, crochet the 4th edge together and you have a matching set!

EDGING

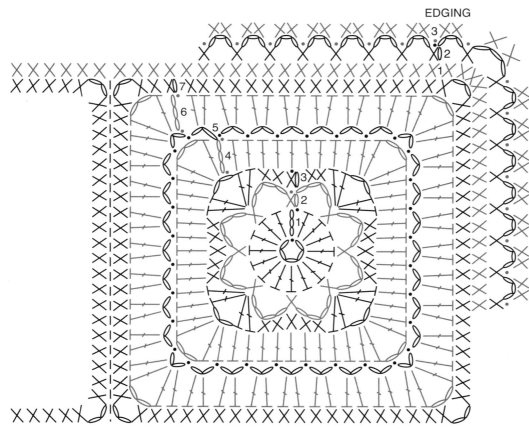

soft and comfy throw

Materials

Yarn 🟦

RED HEART *Designer Sport*, 3oz/85g balls, each approx 279yd/255m (acrylic)
•8 balls #3770 Berry

Crochet hook

Size I/9 (5.5mm) crochet hook *or any size to obtain correct gauge*

Notions

Yarn needle

Finished Measurements

Approx 47"/119.5cm wide x 56"/142cm long

Gauge

1 Square = 9 x 9"/23 x 23cm; Rounds 1–5 = 5" x 5"/12.5cm x 12.5cm using size I/9 (5.5mm) crochet hook.
Remember to check gauge for best results!

How to make a gauge swatch

Work Rounds 1–5 of Square. Resulting gauge swatch should measure approx 5" x 5"/12.5cm x 12.5cm. Adjust hook size if necessary to obtain correct gauge.

Square (make 30)

Ch 4; join with sl st in first ch to form a ring.

Round 1 (right side) Ch 3 (counts as first dc here and throughout), work 15 more dc in ring; join with sl st in top of beginning ch—16 dc.

Round 2 Ch 4 (counts as dc, ch 1 here and throughout), [dc in next dc, ch 1] 15 times; join with sl st in 3rd ch of beginning ch—16 dc and 16 ch-1 sp.

Round 3 Ch 3, 2 dc in next ch-1 sp, [dc in next dc, 2 dc in next ch-1 sp] 15 times; join with sl st in top of beginning ch—48 dc.

Round 4 Ch 1, sc in same st as join, ch 5, sl st in 5th ch from hook (corner made), sk next 2 dc, sc in next dc, ch 2, sk next 2 dc, sc in next dc, ch 3, sk next 2 dc, sc in next dc, ch 2, sk next 2 dc, *sc in next dc, ch 5, sl st in 5th ch from hook (corner made), sk next 2 dc, sc in next dc, ch 2, sk next 2 dc, sc in next dc, ch 3, sk next 2 dc, sc in next dc, ch 2, sk next 2 dc; repeat from * around; join with sl st in first sc.

Round 5 (Sl st, ch 3, 4 dc, ch 3, 5 dc) in first ch-5 sp (beginning corner made), sc in next ch-2 sp, 5 dc in next ch-3 sp, sc in next ch-2 sp, *(5 dc, ch 3, 5 dc) in next ch-5 sp (corner made), sc in next ch-2 sp, 5 dc in next ch-3 sp, sc in next ch-2 sp; repeat from * around; join with sl st in top of beginning ch-3—one 5-dc group and 2 sc along each side, and 4 corners. Fasten off.

Round 6 Join yarn with sl st in any corner ch-3 sp, ch 1, (sc, ch 3, sc) in same ch-3 sp (corner made), ch 5, sk next 5 dc, dc in next sc, ch 3, sk next 2 dc, sc in next dc (center dc of 5-dc group), ch 3, sk next 2 dc, dc in next sc, ch 5, sk next 5 dc, *(sc, ch 3, sc) in next ch-3 sp (corner made), ch 5, sk next 5 dc, dc in next sc, ch 3, sk next 2 dc, sc in next dc, ch 3, sk next 2 dc, dc in next sc, ch 5, sk next 5 dc; repeat from * around; join with sl st in first sc—2 ch-5 sp and 2 ch-3 sp

along each side, and 4 corners.

Round 7 (Sl st, ch 3, 2 dc, ch 2, 3 dc) in first ch-3 sp (beginning corner made), 5 dc in next ch-5 sp, 3 dc in next 2 ch-3 sps, 5 dc in next ch-5 sp, *(3 dc, ch 2, 3 dc) in next ch-3 sp (corner made), 5

dc in next ch-5 sp, 3 dc in next 2 ch-3 sps, 5 dc in next ch-5 sp; repeat from * around; join with sl st in top of beginning ch-3—22 dc along each side, and 4 corner ch-2 sp.

Round 8 Ch 1, hdc in each dc around, working (2 hdc, ch 2, 2 hdc) in each corner ch-2 sp; join with sl st in first hdc—26 hdc along each side, and 4 corner ch-2 sp.

Round 9 Ch 3, dc in each hdc around, working 3 dc in each corner ch-2 sp; join with sl st in top of beginning ch—116 dc. Fasten off.

Finishing

Arrange squares into 6 rows of 5 squares each and sew squares together.

Border

With right side facing, join yarn with sl st in center dc of any corner 3-dc group to work first along short edge.

Round 1 (right side) Ch 1, 2 hdc in same st as join, [hdc in each dc and seam to center dc of next corner 3-dc group, 3 hdc in center dc] 3 times, hdc in each dc to end, work 1 more hdc in same st as join; join with sl st in first hdc.

Round 2 Ch 1, sc in same st as join (center hdc of corner 3-hdc group); ***working along short side, 3 dc in next st, sc in next st, *sk next st, 3 dc in next st, sk next st, sc in next st; repeat from * to next corner 3-hdc group, 3 dc in first hdc of 3-hdc group, sc in center hdc of 3-hdc group; working along long side, 3 dc in next st, sc in next st, **sk next st, 3 dc in next st, sk next st, sc in next st; repeat from ** to 2 sts before next corner 3-hdc group, 3 dc in next st, sc in next st, 3 dc in first hdc of 3-hdc group, sc in center hdc of 3-hdc group; repeat from *** to work along next short and long sides, omitting last sc; join with sl st in first sc. Fasten off.

Weave in all ends.

flower box blanket

Rose Callahan

Materials

Yarn ⑶

RED HEART Designer Sport, 3oz/85g balls, each approx 279yd/255m (acrylic)

2 balls each:
- #3002 Black (A)
- #3410 Granite (B)
- #3770 Berry (C)
- #3601 Cornsilk (D)
- #3261 Terra Cotta (E)
- #3650 Pistachio (F)
- #3515 Lagoon (G)

Crochet hook

Size I/9 (5.5mm) crochet hook *or any size to obtain correct gauge*

Notions

Yarn needle

Finished Measurements

Approx 53½"/136cm x 61"/155.5cm

Gauge

Motif = 7½"/19cm square
Remember to check gauge for best results!

EDGING

MOTIF

Stitch Glossary

rev sc (reverse sc) Working from left to right, insert hook in next specified st to right of last st, yarn over and draw up a loop, yarn over and draw through 2 loops on hook.

Blanket

Motif (make 8 of each color)
With appropriate color, ch 4, join with sl st to form a ring.
Round 1 (right side) Ch 5 (counts as first dc and ch-2 sp); [dc in ring, ch 2] 7 times; join with sl st in 3rd ch of beginning ch-5—8 dc and 8 ch-2 sps.
Round 2 Sl st in next ch-2 sp, ch 1, (sc, ch 1, dc, tr, dc, ch 1, sc) in same ch-2 sp (petal made); *(sc, ch 1, dc, tr, dc, ch 1, sc) in next ch-2 sp (petal made); repeat from * around; join with sl st in first sl st—8 petals.
Round 3 Pulling petals forward and working around post of each dc on round 1, sc around back of post of first dc; *ch 3, sc around back of post of next dc**; ch 5 (corner made), sc around back of post of next dc; repeat from * 3 mores times, ending last repeat at **; ch 2, join with dc in first sc (last corner made)—8 sc, 4 ch-3

sps and 4 corner ch-5 sps.
Round 4 Ch 3 (counts as dc), 2 dc around post of joining dc; *3 dc in next ch-3 sp**; (3 dc, ch 3, 3 dc) in next corner ch-5 sp; repeat from * 3 more times, ending last repeat at **; 3 dc in last corner ch-5 sp; ch 1, join with hdc in 3rd ch of beginning ch-3 (corner ch-3 sp made)—12 groups of 3 dc and 4 corner ch-3 sps.
Round 5 Ch 3 (counts as dc), 2 dc around post of joining hdc; *sk next 3 dc, 3 dc in sp before next 3 dc; repeat from * across to next corner ch-3 sp; sk next 3 dc**; (3 dc, ch 3, 3 dc) in next corner ch-3 sp; repeat from * 3 more times, ending last repeat at **; 3 dc in last corner ch-3 sp; ch 1, join with hdc in 3rd ch of beginning ch-3 (corner ch-3 sp made)—16 groups of 3 dc and 4 corner ch-3 sps.
Round 6 Repeat Round 5—20 groups of 3 dc and 4 corner ch-3 sps.
Round 7 Ch 3 (counts as dc), dc around post of joining hdc; *dc in each dc across to next corner ch-3 sp**; (2 dc, ch 3, 2 dc) in next corner ch-3 sp; repeat from * 3 more times, ending last repeat at **; 2 dc in last corner ch-3 sp; ch 1, join with hdc in 3rd ch of beginning ch-3 (corner ch-3 sp made)—76 dc and 4 corner ch-3 sps.
Round 8 Repeat Round 7—92 dc and 4 corner ch-3 sps. Fasten off.

Assembly

Refer to chart for placement of motifs. Join motifs into 8 rows with 7 motifs in each row as follows: With right sides of 2 motifs tog, working through both thicknesses, join with sl st in back loop of middle ch in corner, sl st in back loop of each ch and dc across to and including middle ch in next corner.
Fasten off.

Edging

Round 1 With right side facing, join C with sl st in any dc, ch 2 (counts as hdc), hdc in each dc around, working 5 hdc in ch-3 sp at each of 4 corners and hdc in each motif joining; join with sl st in 2nd ch of beginning ch-2.

Round 2 Ch 1, sc in same ch as joining; *ch 1, sk next hdc to right of last st, rev sc in next hdc to right of last st; repeat from * around; ch 1, join with sl st in first sc.
Fasten off.

Bobbles

With right side facing, join desired color with sl st around post of hdc at any motif joining on round 1 of edging, ch 3 (counts as dc), 7 dc around post of same hdc—8 dc. Fasten off, leaving an 8"/20cm tail for sewing. With yarn needle, weave tail through top of each dc, pull tight and stitch top tightly to base of dc to form a bobble. Fasten off. Work Bobble at each remaining motif joining and at center of each corner.

Finishing

Weave in all ends.

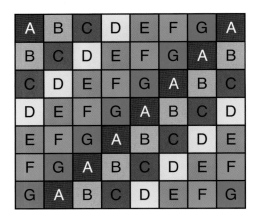

all angles afghan

Materials

Yarn 4️⃣

RED HEART Collage, 3.5oz/100g balls, each approx 218yd/200m (acrylic)
• 6 balls #2350 Blue Wave (A)

RED HEART Super Saver, 7oz/198g skeins, each approx 364yd/333m (acrylic).
2 skeins each:
• #381 Light Blue (B)
• #347 Light Periwinkle (C)
• #885 Delft Blue (D)

Crochet hook
Size J/10 (6mm) crochet hook *or any size to obtain correct gauge*

Notions
• Stitch markers
• Yarn needle

Finished Measurements
Approx 50"/127cm x 74"/187.5cm

Gauge
Rounds 1–3 on Small Granny Square = approx 4¼"/11cm square
Remember to check gauge for best results!

Stitch Glossary

foundation double crochet eyelet (dc eyelet) Ch 3, dc in 3rd ch from hook.
beginning corner shell Work (ch 3, 2 dc, ch 1, 3 dc) in ch-1 sp of **corner shell** or in indicated dc eyelet sp.
corner shell Work (3 dc, ch 1, 3 dc) in ch-1 sp of corner shell.
shell Work 3 dc in indicated ch-1 sp or in indicated dc eyelet sp.

Small Granny Square (with one color)
Square 1A Work 9 rounds with A.
Square 1B Work 9 rounds with B.
Square 1C Work 9 rounds with C.
Square 1D Work 9 rounds with D.

With appropriate color, ch 4; join with sl st to form a ring.
Round 1 (right side) Ch 3 (counts as dc now and throughout), 2 dc in ring (shell made), ch 1; [shell in ring, ch 1] 3 times; join with sl st in 3rd ch of beginning ch-3—4 shells and 4 corner ch-1 sps.
Round 2 Sl st in next 2 dc and in next ch-1 sp, work beginning corner shell in same ch-1 sp, ch 1; [(corner shell, ch 1) in next ch-1 sp] 3 times; join with sl st in 3rd ch of beginning corner shell—4 corner shells. Place marker in ch-1 sp of each corner shell and move up to ch-1 sp of each corner shell on each round as work progresses.
Round 3 Sl st in next 2 dc and in next ch-1 sp, work beginning corner shell, ch 1, (shell, ch 1) in next ch-1 sp; [(corner shell, ch 1) in next corner shell, (shell, ch 1) in next ch-1 sp] 3 times; join—4 corner shells and 4 shells.

Round 4 Sl st in next 2 dc and in next ch-1 sp, work beginning corner shell, ch 1, [(shell, ch 1) in next ch-1 sp] 2 times; *(corner shell, ch 1) in next corner shell, [(shell, ch 1) in next ch-1 sp] 2 times; repeat from * 2 more times; join—4 corner shells and 8 shells.

Rounds 5–9 Work same as round 4, working one more (shell, ch 1) between corner shells on each side of granny square in each round than in previous round. At end of Round 5—4 corner shells and 12 shells. At end of Round 9—4 corner shells and 28 shells. At end of Round 9, fasten off.

REPEAT ROUND 4 AS DIRECTED

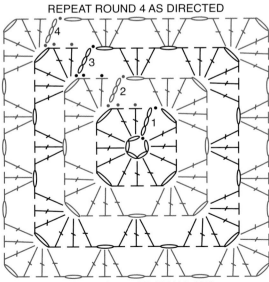

ROUNDS 1-4 OF SMALL AND LARGE GRANNY SQUARES

Small Granny Square (with multiple colors)
Square 2E One round each [A, C, B, D] twice, A
Square 2F One round each [A, D, B, C] twice, A
Work same as Small Granny Square (with one color) except at end of each round, fasten off after joining sl st. With right side facing, join next color with sl st in ch-1 sp of any corner shell and work same as Small Granny Square (with one color), starting with beginning corner shell on Rounds 2–9.

Large Granny Square
Square 3 With A, work same as Small Granny Square (with one color), working 18 rounds instead of 9 rounds. At end of Round 18—4 corner shells and 64 shells.

Small Granny Rectangle
Rectangle 4A Work 9 rounds with A.
Rectangle 4B Work 9 rounds with B.
Rectangle 4C Work 9 rounds with C.
Rectangle 4D Work 9 rounds with D.
Work 10 foundation dc eyelet stitches.
Note Dc eyelet sps have dc on one side and ch-3 sps on other side. See "Starting the Rectangle Grannies" step-by-step at right.
Round 1 Sl st around post of last dc made (dc eyelet sp), work beginning corner shell in same dc eyelet sp, ch 1, (shell, ch 1) in each dc eyelet sp across to last dc eyelet sp, [shell, ch 1] 3 times in last dc eyelet sp; working on opposite side of dc eyelets, sk last eyelet sp worked, (shell, ch 1) in each dc eyelet sp across to last dc eyelet, (shell, ch 1) in last dc eyelet sp; join with sl st in 3rd ch of beginning corner shell—3 shells at each end and 8 shells on each of 2 long sides between ends. Place marker in each ch-1 sp between 3 shells at ends to mark as corner ch-1 sps.
Round 2 Sl st in next 2 dc and in next ch-1 sp, work beginning corner shell in same ch-1 sp, ch 1; *(shell, ch 1) in each ch-1 sp across to next corner ch-1 sp**; (corner shell, ch 1) in each of next 2 corner ch-1 sps; repeat from * to **; (corner shell, ch 1) in last corner ch-1 sp; join with sl st in 3rd ch of beginning corner shell—4 corner shells and 9 shells on each of 2 long sides between corners. Move markers to ch-1 sp of each corner shell and move up to ch-1 sp of each corner shell on each round as work progresses.
Round 3 Sl st in next 2 dc and in next ch-1 sp, work beginning corner shell in same ch-1 sp, ch 1; *(shell, ch 1) in each ch-1 sp across to next corner ch-1 sp, (corner shell, ch 1) in corner ch-1 sp, (shell, ch 1) in next ch-1 sp**; (corner shell, ch 1) in corner ch-1 sp; repeat from * to **; join with sl st in 3rd ch of beginning corner shell—4 corner shells, 10 shells between corners on long sides and 1 shell between corners on short sides.

Rounds 4–9 Work same as Round 3, working one more (shell, ch 1) between corner shells on each side of granny rectangle in each round than in previous round. At end of Round 4—4 corner shells, 11 shells between corners on long sides and 2 shells between corners on short sides. At end of Round 9—4 corner shells, 16 shells between corners on long sides and 7 shells between corners on short sides. At end of Round 9, fasten off.

Large Granny Rectangle

Rectangle 5 Work 18 rounds same as Small Granny Rectangle, changing yarns same as Small Granny Square (with multiple colors) as follows: one round each [A, C, A, B, A, D, A, B] twice, A, C. At end of Round 18—4 corner shells, 25 shells between corners on long sides and 16 shells between corners on short sides. At end of Round 18, fasten off.

Assembly

With right sides facing, pin squares and rectangles together following assembly diagram. With A, working from bottom to top along vertical "seams" with wrong sides of adjacent squares/rectangles tog, join with sl st in corner ch-1 sp on front square/rectangle; *ch 1, sc in same corner ch-1 sp as joining through both thicknesses, ch 1, sk one st on front square/rectangle, sc in next st, ch 1, sk one st on back square/rectangle, sc in next st; repeat from * across to end of this vertical "seam", ending with sc in corner ch-1 sp through both thicknesses. Fasten off. Repeat this for all other vertical "seams". Then, repeat for horizontal "seams."

Edging

Round 1 With right side facing, join A with sl st in any sc near a corner; ch 1, sc in same sc as joining, sc in each sc and ch-1 sp around, working 3 sc in each of 4 corner ch-1 sps on assembled afghan; join with sl st in first sc. Fasten off. Place marker in center sc of 3 sc in each corner and move marker up to center sc in each corner of each round as work progresses.

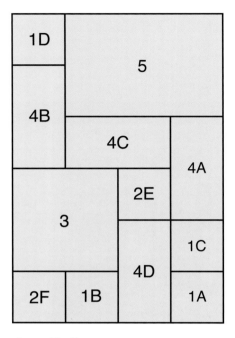

Assembly diagram

Round 2 With right side facing, join D with sl st in first sc, ch 1, sc in same sc as joining, sc in each sc around, working 3 sc in center sc of 3 sc in each corner; join with sl st in first sc. Fasten off.

Rounds 3–5 Repeat Round 2, 3 more times, using B for Round 3, C for Round 4 and A for Round 5.

Finishing

Weave in all ends.

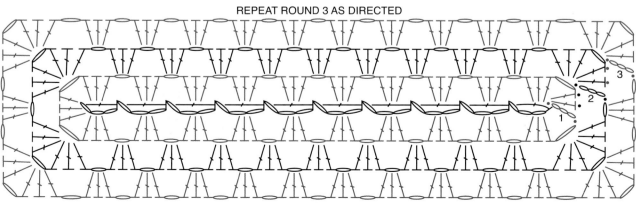

REPEAT ROUND 3 AS DIRECTED

ROUNDS 1-3 OF SMALL AND LARGE GRANNY RECTANGLES

grannies on point

Materials

Yarn (4)

TLC Essentials, 6oz/170g skeins, each approx 312yd/285m (acrylic) 1 skein each:

- #2615 Light Celery (A)
- #2254 Persimmon (B)
- #2220 Butter (C)
- #2936 Claret (D)
- #2531 Light Plum (E)

Crochet hook

Size H/8 (5mm) crochet hook *or any size to obtain correct gauge*

Notions

- 14"/35.5cm square pillow form
- Yarn needle

Finished Measurements

14"/35.5cm square

Gauge

Rounds 1–3 of Granny Square = 4"/10cm square *Remember to check gauge for best results!*

Rose Callahan

Stitch Glossary

beginning corner shell Work (ch 3, 2 dc, ch 1, 3 dc) in sp indicated.
corner shell Work (3 dc, ch 1, 3 dc) in sp indicated.
shell Work 3 dc in sp indicated.

Pillow #1

Granny Square (make 4)
With A, ch 4; join with sl st to form a ring.

Round 1 (right side) Ch 3 (counts as dc), 2 dc in ring, ch 1 [shell in ring, ch 1] 3 times; join with sl st in 3rd ch of beginning ch-3—4 shells and 4 corner ch-1 sps. Fasten off.

Round 2 With right side facing, join B with sl st in next ch-1 sp, work beginning corner shell in same ch-1 sp as joining, ch 1, [corner shell in next ch-1 sp, ch 1] 3 times; join with sl st in 3rd ch of beginning corner shell—4 corner shells. Fasten off.

Round 3 With right side facing, join C with sl st in ch-1 sp of next corner shell, work beginning corner shell in same ch-1 sp as joining, ch 1, shell in next ch-1 sp, ch 1, [corner shell in ch-1 sp of next corner shell, ch 1, shell in next ch-1 sp, ch 1] 3 times; join—4 corner shells and 4 shells. Fasten off.

Round 4 With right side facing, join D with sl st in ch-1 sp of next corner shell, work beginning corner shell in same ch-1 sp as joining, ch 1, [shell in next ch-1 sp, ch 1] 2 times; *corner shell in ch-1 sp of next corner shell, ch 1, [shell in next ch-1 sp, ch 1] 2 times; repeat from * 2 more times; join—4 corner shells and 8 shells. Fasten off.

Rounds 5–8 Work same as Round 4, changing colors in each round and working one more (shell in next ch-1 sp, ch 1) between corner shells on each side of granny square in each round, so that you have a total of 4 more shells in each round than in previous round. At end of Round 8—4 corner shells and 24 shells. Work Round 5 with E, Round 6 with A, Round 7 with B and Round 8 with C.

Pillow #2

Granny Square (make 4)
Work same as pillow #1, using color sequence as follows: Round

GRANNY SQUARE

1 with C, Round 2 with B, Round 3 with A, Round 4 with E, Round 5 with D, Round 6 with C, Round 7 with B, Round 8 with A.

Assembly

With right sides facing, arrange 4 squares into 2 rows with 2 squares in each row. Using C for pillow #1 and A for pillow #2, whipstitch back loops of squares tog, working twice in ch at corners to add strength to corners. Turn joined squares over to wrong side. Bring all 4 corners of joined squares tog to meet in center. Whipstitch back loops of 3 squares tog, leaving last square unjoined. Joined squares should look like an envelope. Insert pillow form into "envelope" between front and back sides of pillow and whipstitch back loops of remaining squares tog.

Finishing

Weave in all ends.